Campfire Leadership

Effective leadership from a personality perspective

Rob Jackson

PRIZM

ISBN: 978-0-9893134-0-7 (print)

ISBN: 978-0-9893134-1-4 (ebook)

DEDICATION

First and foremost, I want to thank my Dad, Lloyd Jackson, for all of the great memories growing up. And thanks for raising & loving me when you didn't have to. My loving, supportive wife, April, and our three adult children: James, Katie and Robert, Jr. Also to my mother and siblings, Ken, Russ, and Nikki.

My forever best friend, Kenny Price, and his fantastic Price & Love families in South Carolina. Treasured friends and encouragers: Jim Dougherty, Syndee Van Gelder, David & Lesley Brandli, Andre Harris, Kirk Huntzinger, Steve Sweeney, Colette & Jim Johnston, Chris McNeaney, Frank Beck and Ray & Dawn Summeier.

Campfire Leaders who influenced this book: Johannes Tysse, Larry Ostendorf, Lyn White, and Bobbie Keen.

Supportive organizations: Leadership Hancock County, and the Future Farmers of America® (FFA) for their commitment to empowering future leaders.

Azamara Club Cruises®, Mosaic Café®, Cabaret Lounge® and Looking Glass® are Trademarks of Royal Caribbean Cruises Ltd. Used with permission.

Editor: Mike Valentino

Cover Design: vaanigraphics.com

Published by: Prizm Management, L.L.C.

i

CONTENTS

FORWARD

When I was 13 years old I lived with my father, who was in the Army and stationed in Anchorage, Alaska. During the summer months, we would spend most of our weekends fishing on the Kenai River. This was in the Kenai Peninsula, just south of our home in Anchorage. My father would fish for king salmon on the river and my brothers and I would fish for trout in the stream that flowed into the river. Those were some of the greatest years of my life!

After spending a long day of fishing and goofing around, we would always end up at the campground's nightly campfire. We would spend hours listening to the fishing stories of the adults who almost landed the 'big one' while fishing that day. They were great stories about adventure and the perils of living in Alaska. The leadership I learned from those men around that campfire would prove to be invaluable later in life.

Years later, I find that I want to be the kind of leader that I saw in those men. They gave such great advice and insight during those nights just sitting around those campfires. I was drawn to their leadership and realized that there were four basic styles of leadership: the Torch leader, Disco Light leader, Spotlight leader and Lighthouse leader. Each of these exhibit myriads of strengths and weaknesses and only when a balance of all four styles meet do we have a truly enlightened leader, the Campfire Leader.

CALL ME REX

When I graduated from college I was proud to have worked hard and graduate near the top of my class. My future looked bright. I figured that all sort of doors would open for me, and they did. I landed a job at a major marketing firm in Boston where I was for several years. At first, everything was going great. Though I was a newbie, I was given some important assignments, and I must say it seemed like I was firing on all cylinders.

But without me realizing it at first, I went into sort of a slump. I'm not sure exactly what went wrong, but I felt like something just wasn't "clicking" anymore at my job. I understood that what I was going through basically involved "communication challenges." To correct the problem, I tried some online seminars but, honestly, they just didn't seem to help very much.

It all seemed easy when I was a little younger. In college I never had any problem communicating with people, and I could always "read" people like a book. Despite my success and my experience, had become much more difficult, and I'd begun to wonder, am I doing something wrong? I spoke with the head of HR about it and she suggested that I get in contact with a man named Rex Lloyd, an older gentleman who had once helped out a friend of his in a big way when this friend needed some career counseling. I was a bit reluctant at first, but one Wednesday afternoon when the day seemed to be dragging on interminably and nothing was going right, I picked up the phone and called.

I was surprised by how helpful Mr. Lloyd was to me, a complete stranger. "Please call me Rex," he insisted when I kept addressing him as Mister. I reciprocated and asked him to call me Jim (my full name is Jim Knight). He told me that he wanted to teach me about "four different types of communications styles" and suggested that we meet for brunch over the weekend. Intrigued, I readily accepted his invitation.

It was a fine April morning, the warm sunshine tending to make the waning and harsh Yankee winter a bad memory. It was Saturday morning so the drive was easy and I arrived early for the meeting, but not as early as Rex did. He already had a table waiting and he waved me in when I walked into the crowded restaurant. As I sat down I asked, "How did you know it was me?"

The older man (I guessed from his salt and pepper beard that he was in his early sixties) just looked smart. He smiled and said, "You came in alone and your eyes appeared inquisitive. Also, people your age typically don't dine alone."

"You must be a very smart man," I said, hoping that it didn't come off as patronizing.

"I find few geniuses in life," he noted, "but I do find people who watch life go by them and may even be able to describe what they saw. Far rarer, however, are people who observe and draw conclusions -- right or wrong -- from life."

Don't ask me how, but he managed to say it in a way that didn't make him sound like a smart aleck, but just observant, which helped to build up my trust in him almost immediately.

"You seem to have a pretty good read on people," I said.

After the bare minimum of small talk, Rex got straight to the business at hand. "Jim, if you want to advance in your career, as well as in life in general, you need to become what I like to call a Campfire leader."

That one caught me by surprise. Rex didn't seem like the kind of new age mumbo-jumbo kind of guy.

I said, "I'm not sure I'm following you."

He held eye contact with me and said, "I know that you're not, at least not yet, but the concept is actually quite simple once you learn to identify it. You see, there are basically four different kinds of leaders. Each has its own set of characteristics. All of us have at least some of these characteristics, but one of the different leadership types is predominant within each individual."

Wow! That was a mouthful. It made sense, but it was a lot to absorb, and the twinkle in Rex's eye told me that he knew I was having trouble processing everything that he had just said.

"Don't worry, Jim," he said reassuringly, "like I said, people learn best through observation. That's why I want to show you examples of each of the four leadership styles. Not from some book or a CD, but from actual people who we are going to interact with."

I liked the sound of that. I'm more of a "hands on" kind of person so this approach sounded like it would be right up my alley.

Rex reached into the pocket of the sports jacket and wrote down an address on the back of his business card. "Meet me here at nine o'clock sharp on Monday morning," he said.

I took the card, noted the address and put it in my wallet. "You're on," I said, and Rex skillfully shifted the subject to the breakfast menu.

TYPES OF LIGHTS

After ordering our coffee and omelets, Rex began again. "Now, these are stereotypes and I'm describing the EXTREME case of each type. But I have to do this in order for you to make the distinction between the Leadership styles. Most people are 'blends' of one or more styles and some people are combinations of more than... Well now, I'm getting ahead of myself. "He smiled. " Let's start with the basics:

A Torch Leader is a leader by title alone. They really don't show many leadership qualities in the way that they lead. Many tend to be meek, timid, and lack the confidence. And, just like a torch, they only shine enough light to see just enough ahead to really wonder where they're going. I always felt sorry for these kinds of leaders because they never really seemed to want to be in charge. They were just too nice to say no when they had the position appointed to them. It's hard to follow these leaders. They are very likeable, but don't seem to have a clear direction or passion for leadership.

The Spot Light Leader is easy to recognize, or should I say 'hear' because you can't miss them! They will remind you over and over that they are the leader. They often possess an "in your face" style of leadership. Not one of leadership abilities, but of verbosity and intimidation. They look for ways to put the focus on them, even at your expense. It's hard to like and very difficult to follow this style of leader for extended periods. They do not have a passion for leadership, only drive for power and authority.

The Disco Light Leader is also easy to identify due to their talkative, animated nature and desire to be the center of influence or attention. Sometimes it's hard to determine if they are leading or performing! We call them the Disco light because they like attention on themselves and others. Storytelling and giving examples come very naturally to these expressive personalities and they have the gift of gab. Leadership style tends to be more in groups, rather than individuals due to their desire to influence and motivate crowds. We like to follow Disco Light leaders because of their heavy praise, fun attitudes and encouragement.

The Lighthouse Leader is much like a true lighthouse, always warning of impending doom. This analytical leader focuses more on empirical data over interpersonal skills. They don't like attention drawn upon them and are much more comfortable in one-on-one settings. But in reality this individual would prefer not to communicate verbally at all – they are more comfortable with written communication where they can be precise and detailed. They constantly strive for perfection for themselves and often expect it from others.

This was a lot of information to digest! But as I drove home I realized how excited I was to begin this journey with Rex. I had a feeling that somehow this was going to change me and help me grow in my relationships and sure enough, it was only the beginning.

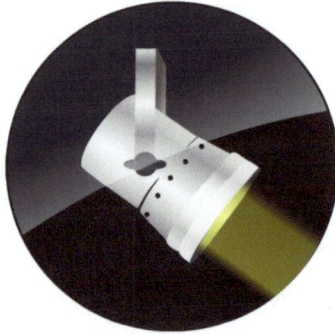

SPOT LIGHT LEADER

Monday morning seemed to arrive in no time, and I met Rex in the lobby of a large office building in Waltham, a bustling suburb of Boston. He shook hands with me and introduced me to a tall man wearing tan slacks and a white shirt with his sleeves rolled up. The man had a strong jaw and a cleanly shaved head. "Jim, this is Jake Simpson, he's a Project Manager for Cooper & Bigelow, a mid-sized architectural firm."

Greeting me with a firm handshake, Simpson said, "Soon to be larger than mid-sized," and winked at Rex.

"Nice to meet you," I said, not exactly sure what to make of this guy.

"Have you ever been to a construction site, Jim?" he asked.

I shook my head no.

"Good," he said, picking up some blueprints. "There's a first time for everything. Let's go."

We followed him to his black Chevy pick-up and off we went. During the ten-minute drive, as Rex and I remained mostly quiet, we listened as Simpson took three phone calls. On each one (from what we could hear on our end) it appeared that his underlings at the work site had questions for him. His answers seemed firm and direct. He wasn't really engaging in conversation as much as he was issuing orders and explaining what it was that he wanted done. I looked over at Rex as we drove along and he seemed mildly amused.

The work site was a partially completed strip mall on a busy stretch of State Highway 20. As soon as we arrived, Simpson walked straight over to the supervisor in charge of the work crew. "Problem with one of the vendors, Henry?" he asked.

Henry was a middle-aged man with a hint of a pot belly and a bushy moustache. "That's an understatement, Jake. Of all things it's the plumbing supply company. They delivered the wrong pipe fittings, meaning the basic plumbing installation for the one whole wing will have to be delayed."

Simpson shook his head and said, "Not acceptable." Then he ushered Henry over to his truck, where he spread out some blueprints on the hood. "See here, its right in the specs. And the work order that went to the plumbing supply company has an exact copy of this, so what excuse do they have?"

Henry shrugged. "Honestly, I don't really know. They didn't give a reason; they just said it will take two weeks before they can deliver the right fittings."

Rolling up the blueprints, Simpson turned to Mr. Lloyd and said, "See, Rex? What do I always say? If you want something done right you have to do it yourself."

I watched as Jake Simpson stood with the early morning

sunshine reflecting brightly off of his bald head. His blue eyes were filled with determination as he fished his cell phone from his pocket. He pressed a few buttons and was soon on the phone with the plumbing supply company. I heard him ask about the mistake, and he listened (not too patiently) to their reply. "Well look," he intoned, his voice firm, "I know that computer errors happen. But a screw-up on your end should not become a mess that we have to clean up on this end. Two weeks will put our project way behind schedule. Two days is the most that we can afford, and I'm hoping I'm being clear on that."

After a few more words from the person on the other end, Simpson nodded and said, "Good, that's more like it."

After he hung up, I asked him if the problem had been solved. His mood seemed to lighten up a little bit. "As a matter of fact it has, kid. You see, it's just a matter of being persistent. Henry is very good at what he does here on the job site, but when something goes wrong, he's not a good troubleshooter. That's what I've been doing for over fifteen years now. I think it's all about being blunt and letting people know in no uncertain terms exactly what it is that you expect of them."

As we walked through the construction site, stepping over exposed cables and other equipment a few steps behind Simpson, Rex said, "Jim, what you're seeing in our friend Jake is a classic example of a Spot Light type personality in action."

I thought I was starting to understand. I said, "You mean because he's driven to succeed?"

"Yes, that's part of it," Rex replied. "But there's more. The Driver's main characteristic and what makes him a Driver is that he always has the whole picture firmly in mind. Everything he does, like delegating work, insisting on production and stimulating activity is done with that whole picture front and center in his frame of mind."

No doubt about it, Rex certainly knew what he was talking about. Throughout the day I witnessed numerous examples of what made Jake Simpson the classic Driver type. For instance, later in the morning the electrical contractor approached him with a problem. Apparently, there was a company rule that an apprentice had to have at least one year of training before working on a job site. It turned out that one individual was short a couple of months and this was holding up the job. Rex and I were close enough to hear when the Company Rep, a whippet thin guy named Slim, and Jake talked. We heard the Rep relay the problem. Slim seemed ready to walk away when Jake didn't immediately respond. Jake said, "Just a minute there, Slim. I can't let that problem hold up my project. We have a deadline and commitments."

Slim started, "Listen I'm not sure what to tell ya."

"Well Slim, I can tell you what you already know. I can't get involved in internal problems on the one hand. On the other hand I can't, and I repeat I CAN'T let this slow down my schedule."

"Well, listen," the Rep retorted. "I dunno what to tell you."

"Look, Slim. How long have you been in this position?"

Slim's eyes shifted a bit, and narrowed. He was wary. "Well, about six months I guess now. Why?"

"Well, basically you're a new man and I'm an old pro. Let me give you some advice. There are solutions to any problem. And there is a solution to this one. It's up to you, not me, to find it. All I can tell you is there is going to be hell to pay if this holds up our project. This isn't such a tough problem. It's a matter of finding a different man for the job. Am I right?"

Slim stuffed his hands into his jean's pockets. "Yeah, I guess so."

Jake smiled, but it wasn't a friendly smile. "Then find him. And fast."

We returned to the Cooper & Bigelow architectural firm towards the end of the afternoon. As we entered the lobby, Simpson walked up to the receptionist, a lovely red-haired girl named Sheila. "Messages?" he asked.

Sheila said, "Yes, your wife called."

Jake turned to us. "Excuse me guys. I'll be right back with ya." Again we stood off close enough to hear, although we didn't intend to eavesdrop. He called his wife and listened carefully. When he spoke his voice was firm. "No, babe, there's nothing to discuss. It's not an option, no daughter of mine is going to get a tattoo. No matter where on her body it is and no matter how cute and pretty she thinks it is. Period."

He wasn't smiling when he got back to us but he wasn't frowning either. His lips were tight with determination.

Driving home through the thick rush hour traffic of Route 128, I reflected on the valuable lessons I'd learned today. I learned that there were four different kinds of leaders, all with slightly different characteristics, strengths and weaknesses. I saw Jake Simpson, who was a Spot Light type leader in action. His strengths in dealing with problems were illustrated by a plumbing supply problem. Spot Lights are goal oriented and always keep their eyes on the big picture. They don't let small problems hold them up. When the plumbing supply company suggested they needed two weeks to straighten out a problem, Jake, in turn, would not allow it. It was a practical solution in that the supply company just wanted a comfortable time frame to correct their problem. Jake did not, would not, go along with it. He demanded they fix it in a much shorter time span. They didn't have much choice but to comply or face the implied risk, i.e., lose the job.

Later he handled another problem with an apprentice. Knowing he couldn't interfere in the company's internal problems he gave the Rep the understanding that it was his problem and he had to solve it. He therefore motivated the Rep to find a solution. At times he comes on strong and sometimes appears to be inflexible. Of course, sometimes this type of approach doesn't work and in certain instances could even be counterproductive.

But today was just the tip of the iceberg. Rex had me more curious than ever about the other leader styles. I wonder which one we would explore next time?

LIGHTHOUSE LEADER

A few days later I learned the answer. Rex told me about Syndee Crewson, an Accounting Manager of a video gaming company called Playtime. I remember reading about them in the Business Journal, this state of the art venture had posted record growth for two consecutive years.

We had a meeting set up. She had some unique leadership and management problems. I met Rex in the lobby of the Prudential Tower in downtown Boston. We took the escalator up to Ms. Crewson's floor.

When we were ushered into her office, she said, "You're three minutes early but I'm ready for you. I've allotted forty five minutes for this interview. Thanks for sending the questions ahead of time so I could prepare."

The comment fit her appearance. Her hair was cut in a short bob, but long enough to flatter her classic features. Her navy suit fit perfectly. She wore a beautiful broach on her scarf which gave her a super sharp appearance although they had not been in fashion for several years.

Rex said, "I thought it would be helpful. I know I like to be fully prepared myself."

Syndee glanced at the clock and then began studying a sheet of paper before her. She looked up at us and asked, "You asked about my leadership strengths." She paused to think. "I have a few, but frankly I feel that I have more shortcomings as a leader. One of the things that frustrate me most is inaccuracies or errors. I don't understand how, if someone is diligent, their work would be full of errors and or inaccurate information. It gets me so upset it sometimes throws me off balance I and I don't exercise my usual judgment."

Rex and I exchanged a knowing glance. This was something he and I had been discussing earlier in a casual conversation. Syndee looked at us expectantly, waiting for an explanation.

"You've heard of the dumbing down of America?" Rex asked, letting her in our private little joke.

The Accounting Manager frowned. "I'm afraid so."

Rex said, "It's a sad fact. Our nation is way down on the totem pole of advanced academics vis a vis other competing countries. We've even fallen behind China in some scientific areas, though not so very long ago we were decades ahead of them. It's a complex situation, of course, but much of it, I believe, comes from people no longer caring about excellence."

"That's only one small part of the problem," she insisted. "More to the point is the fact that people don't pay attention to details. They think, 'let someone else worry about the small things – it's not my job.' Well, I'm here to tell you that's a surefire recipe for failure. Details do indeed matter. In fact, I would contend that paying strict attention to even the smallest details, along with being highly organized, are the most important components of any job. But people just don't see it that way anymore, especially younger people. I guess, unfortunately, they were just brought up differently."

Trying to steer the conversation in a more positive direction,

Rex asked, "What would you say was your 'finest moment?'"

Finally we got a grin from our rather reserved host. "Ah, we all hope to have one or two of those. Don't we?"

We both just nodded politely.

"Well, I'd say my crowning achievement was when I warned of an impending financial crisis and was promptly told that I was being too cautious and conservative. I held my ground even though others tried to brush it off. As it turned out, I was right."

"That must make you feel good," I said. "Now tell me about some challenges you face as a leader."

She thought for a moment, choosing her words carefully. "I find change to be quite difficult. It requires advanced planning and patient consideration before taking that first step. But sometimes when I try to communicate these concepts to people, they feel that I'm being unnecessarily dour. I've actually been told on more than one occasion that I don't have enough charisma or enthusiasm."

Rex propped his left foot up onto his right knee. "In some cases of business leadership that isn't required. It's best left to someone to whom it comes naturally."

I then asked, "As I understand it, your company is primarily in the business of creating video games of all types, but mostly action adventure games, and now you're making forays into new foreign markets."

"Yes," Syndee replied, looking somewhat impressed that I'd done my homework. "And the problem is that we are considering expanding into Europe, starting with the German market first. It is the EU country with the most disposable income, so it is a natural target for us. In fact, we are soon to have an important meeting regarding this new proposition, but frankly I don't expect to have much to say at the meeting. I will be there mostly in case a financial problem arises. Which is fine with me, I don't like talking much anyway. I do best taking notes."

"Makes sense," Rex said.

Syndee glanced at the wall clock. She stood up and said, "You are free to come with me and observe."

"That's what we're here for," Rex said with a smile.

At the meeting, Rex and I sat in the back of the conference room. It was break time and we were glad that the secretary remembered us and offered us coffee and pastries along with the others.

The German representative commenced the meeting by introducing himself and his colleague. His name was Ernest Smitka, he had graying hair, and of the two he spoke English best. The other German, Dietrich Walheimer, was a shorter blond man with a short, trimmed beard. Smitka opened the comments. He spoke English very well. If it wasn't for the occasional "Z" sounds you could hardly recognize that English wasn't his first language.

He started out, "Our first concern and it is probably going to be the basis for other concerns in the future is this first game being introduced. You call it 'High Noon.' Like all modern video games, it begins with a premise, a 'back story' if you will. In this case, it involves a lone Western Sheriff up against a gang of gunmen. The theme is that nobody in town wants to help him. It's not that they don't like the Sheriff, but they are terrified. The bad guys are professional gunmen and the town has become so peaceful over the years that, at first at least, no one wanted to join a posse and help the Sheriff."

The German executives did not seem overly pleased.

One of the Playtime executives blurted, "You've got to admit it's a great game. It sets up all kinds of ways that the bad guys can "do in" the good guy, and a good player will help the good guy win. We feel it will go over great in your country."

The two Germans exchanged a look which was basically undiscerning.

One of the more exuberant of the Playtime execs, Sherry McDonald, an attractive redhead asked, "What is it that you gentlemen doubt? Is it the number of options which would allow the good guys to win. Or do you feel the game is rigged against the lone good guy?"

The Germans remained stoic but looked like they were thinking.

This was when Syndee stepped in. She said, "If you gentlemen would allow me an observation." Everyone nodded. Syndee said, "Is it not true that what we have here is not a technical or manufacturing or cost problem, but what we have is in actuality a cultural problem?"

Smitka's eyes lit up. "Yes, ma'am, you have -- how do you say -- hit the nail."

Everyone grinned. Syndee went on. "As I understand the German culture from my college internship days in Berlin, it would be illogical and even insane for one man to stand up to a gang of ruthless outlaws. Keep in mind this is not a Super Hero game, this is a game of ordinary people faced with ordinary choices. Should the Sheriff, if he has the chance, shoot one of the desperadoes in the back? Would that be immoral or not in the code of the West? Worse still, and the overriding problem in the German mind, would be why would a man take on such impossible odds. It is illogical. It makes no sense. He has no chance of winning."

"So," Sherry McDonald said, "it's a matter of marketing to make the German consumer understand the American principles that would make such a game a typical display of good over evil in a way that is culturally relevant."

Mr. Smitka smiled at her. "That's our concern."

"Well," piped in another Playtime exec, "I think there are ways we can overcome this. I can think of a few."

Walheimer turned to him. "Could you suggest one, sir?"

"Uh. Yes. Well, I haven't really thought it out yet but it would have something to do with educating the German public."

Both Germans frowned.

The executive, seeing his blunder said, "Don't worry, we have a department full of PR and Advertising guys who will figure that out."

Syndee came back into the conversation. "The point is, people, I don't feel that this is an insurmountable problem. I believe if we were selling this game in the UK we'd have the same kind of problems."

"And even more so in, say, Japan," someone else added.

The Germans nodded and exchanged glances that seemed to suggest that they were willing to help out with bridging the cultural gap. Everyone in the room understood now that to open up foreign markets, certain adjustments would be necessary to make it palatable to different cultures. After all, not everyone overseas completely "gets it" when it comes to understanding the legends and lore of the American "Old West".

When the meeting broke up there seemed to be good feelings for success all around. It was just that several rounds of brainstorming would now have to take place.

While we waited for Syndee to make a phone call in her office Rex and I critiqued the meeting.

He asked me, "What was the most striking thing about the conference to you?"

"Well, it seemed that until Syndee identified the problem, everybody was an expert. But if it wasn't for her analytical thinking none of them would have put a finger on the problem. Definitely not off the top of their heads."

"And she was really just there as an observer," Rex noted. "Most of this was outside of her precise job function, but her analytical leadership style seemed to have left her no choice other than to jump in where she saw the others failing because of their shallow perspective."

Rex and I were scheduled to have lunch with Syndee and probably engage in more discussion about the meeting. She mentioned that she was having lunch in the lobby café with her son and offered for us to join them. We gratefully accepted.

Syndee's son Cory turned out to be much like his mother in his thinking except the teenager was of a generation that didn't take everything quite so seriously.

At one point Syndee asked her son, "So how did the scholarship meeting go?"

Cory finished a bite of his BLT and wiped his lip with a napkin before answering. "Looks good, Mom. The only thing is I might not have hit that calculus as hard as I should. They said something about if I get a tutor, I would be in."

Syndee looked ambivalent. "Did I not warn you about the importance of calculus?"

"Yeah you did, Mom. But don't sweat it. I think I'm in."

I could tell that while Cory seemed pleased with the way things went his mother was not. Syndee was clearly still a bit miffed by her son's breezy attitude. But most of all I got the impression that she was displeased that her son wasn't fully prepared. Without saying it out loud, her overall demeanor seemed to be one of, *something like this would have never happened to me.*

Cory arose quickly and left some money on the table. "I think my parking meter's over time. Gotta run."

When he left, his mother glanced at the money her son had left on the table. Then she checked her watch. "Over tipping. As usual. I don't know what is with these young people today. No appreciation for money."

Our conversation then returned to the board meeting. Rex said, "One of your co-workers really shot from the hip when he said he had ideas in mind to bridge the cultural gap. Then when asked..."

Syndee interrupted. "You are correct -- he had nothing. No ideas at all. You see, he hadn't prepared. It made us look like a bunch of amateurs; and we're not." Then she added, with one of her few smiles of the day, "for the most part."

DISCO LIGHT LEADER

About a week later, Mr. Lloyd set up our third encounter. This time it was an Advertising Account Executive named Nikki Cortez that we were going to spend some time observing. Rex had told me that she was a family friend who exhibited a classically expressive "Disco Light" leadership style. She'd been a top producer for a large advertising agency in Boston for several years. Their offices were on one of the top three floors of the Hancock Tower, in the city's busy downtown area. This glass and steel behemoth had overtaken the Prudential as the Hub's tallest building several decades ago.

Rex and I chatted in the lobby downstairs for a few minutes while waiting for the elevator.

"So this leadership style will be a lot different from the Driver and the Analytical, I'm assuming," I said thinking I already knew the answer.

"Yes and no," Rex said, as always giving a thoughtful reply. "As you will soon discover, there are indeed stark differences. On the other hand, as with all of the leadership styles, there is a certain amount of overlap as well."

"Oh, I get it," I said. "Compare and contrast. Sort of like the ways professors have you approach essays in college."

With a wry smile, Rex said, "Something like that. But of course, there's only so much that I can explain by talking. We learn much more by observing."

I stood up. "Then I guess we're on the next elevator," I said.

A few minutes later, we stepped out of the elevator on the 60th floor, which opened up into a reception area for "Highlights Marketing." A sleek blonde receptionist immediately took note of our arrival and asked if we had an appointment. We told her that we were here to see Nikki Cortez. The receptionist checked her computer, nodded, and directed us to one of the inner offices.

While waiting for Ms. Cortez, we wandered the area gazing at the artwork on the walls which made the room look like a high school boy's bedroom. It was a pop culture paradise with multi colored modern type images. I had to study them to depict the point it was making or trying to make. There were also large poster type pictures of different products ranging from cereal to the latest high-tech gadgets. The energy in the place was palpable. From where we waited we could see the dash and scramble in the inner office cubicles.

When we reached the office, the door was open and Nikki was behind her desk and on the phone chattering in an animated way. She looked up, flashed a quick smile, and put her hand over the phone mouthpiece. "Gentlemen, please have a seat," she said quickly before returning to her call with a "Sorry about that."

When she got off the phone she popped up from her desk and hurried to the door. "Coffee, gentlemen?" she said over her shoulder. We gave our preferences and she returned to her desk. With a sigh she said, "So, here's the story. We're going to be having a sales meeting with all six of our salesmen. The only one missing will be our international guy so I'm taping everything to send him a copy."

"Fine," Rex said.

"I hope you won't be bored with a lot of stuff you know nothing about?" Her eyes darted from me to Rex and back, before she went on. "What I do in our sales meetings is ask each person to be candid with a problem they're currently having in landing a new account. There's nothing at all about the progress the account is making with a campaign we already have or are designing for them. So again it's just current sales problems serious enough to lose the sale."

When the sales force filed into the conference room Rex and I sat as unobtrusively as possible in the back of the room. I whispered to Rex, "I feel like I'm auditing a course in college."

"Maybe you are," he said with a smile.

The sales force was predominantly young. I didn't see anyone over their early thirties.

Nikki, the typical salesperson started off with some wise cracks and jokes that really were inside jokes. Rex and I simply smiled politely.

The first man up was a thirtyish blonde guy, Brian. In California, he would have been considered a surfer dude. But he wasn't cheerful, his firm mouth said so. He started out with a frustrated account. He said, "I'm so close to landing this account but the CEO is resisting my approach."

"What is your approach, Brian?" Nikki asked.

"Well, like we've been taught I'm trying to play to our strength, which is that this agency is one of the best, and what we do best is film. Let me describe the situation."

"As you know Oat Delights is a cereal company. It's been around for eons. The CEO's father or maybe it was his grandfather started the company. Their beginning form of advertising was print. Eventually they realized that film was important too. So they got into it. You've seen their ads. Boring, flat and not very effective. More or less just a way to keep their name out there. Well I did my homework on the demographics and the problem is a two-edged sword. On the one hand you can't say they are hot in one particular demographic or region. They're universal, all over the place with no specific target areas."

Nikki said, "You're right, Brian. That's the good part. Now what's the problem?"

"Well I figure I could substantially increase their sales with a great commercial campaign in the major markets. I'm standing; pitching my guts out, telling them what I suggest is a commercial where we can build the main character into a series. You know like those high-priced celebrity endorsers? They don't even have to show their faces. We know their voices and they still make bank! Even the little lizard guy, what's his name, with the insurance company? You know their success and it's because people become familiar with them. They are funny, they are witty. Let's face it, they sell the product."

All eyes in the room are on Brian, expectant. But Brian seems to be out of speed.

Nikki says, "So they're not buying it. Got any idea why not?"

"Yeah, I do. They are a bunch of old fogies who for years have been content with their position in the marketplace but now others are starting to make inroads into the cereal market. Today it's not just what's yummy, but the emphasis is on healthy and yummy. You know how big that is. Even the White House is into it. But as far as I can figure, they're not interested in film because print has always done it for them and they are not progressive thinkers."

Nikki seemed a bit impatient now. "So you know you have to sell them. If they want print, give it to them. Do you think we can come up with a decent print campaign?"

"Yeah, sure I do. But weren't we always taught to go the distance? Get an account and keep them for years? I could probably sell them on print. After all, we're one of the best ad houses in the country. But I know that with film we could make them fly and have them for years."

Rex turned to me and whispered, "Nothing a salesman likes better than a steady account for years to come."

"You're talking about a cash cow."

"That I am."

Nikki put the question out to the group. "Anybody got any ideas about how to help Brian join us in Cabo san Lucas with the other high scorers? Remember last year in Hawaii? Old Brian here was the hit of the party. Remember that midnight soiree in the big pool? Balancing a martini on his head as he back stroked right like he was trying out for the Olympics."

Everybody laughed, except for one young woman who blushed. As she surveyed the room Nikki noticed and with a laugh said, "Oh that's right, Megan, you weren't here last year. Well, don't worry, this year is going to be even better. I know that the brass here at times is a bit stuffy. They think that Hawaii makes for a wild sales conference destination. Or even Vegas, which is now like Disneyworld. Well, you'll all be glad we'll be going to Cabo. Now that's a happening place."

Everybody applauded. When the room returned to quiet the question that hung in the air was what advice to give to Brian. Nobody had any. They all knew what was at stake. Brian could lose the whole account, or at best come up with a print campaign that he had little confidence in despite the talent of the Highlights marketing creative crew. One consideration that Nikki had to make was the cereal company was already substantial and didn't need much to get them ahead of last year's sales. So she wasn't about to encourage Brian to shoot for the sky.

Nikki said, "Brian, if you don't mind me using a well-worn cliché, I have a feeling that in this case a bird in the hand is better than two in the bush. If you don't go for the print campaign that they seem to prefer, you might wind up with nothing. Better to go with that."

Brian dropped his head. "That's a shame. I even have some ideas that I would of course knock around with the creative types about who the character should be."

Although we had already had coffee, Nikki announced a break and she dashed off somewhere leaving Rex and me alone in the room. I turned to him and said, "Seems like Brian is being muzzled, doesn't it?"

"Yes, I agree," Rex said, "but it's a tough market out there these days and every company is scrambling for whatever they can get."

"Well what I was driving at was, why doesn't Nikki find some way to let Brian try to sell these guys on what he is confident will work?"

"Whatever her leadership style, Nikki is responsible to the brass for sales. And from her perspective a mediocre print campaign that doesn't produce much is better than a progressive looking commercial on TV that might not even be selected. But that might have terrific potential. That's where Nikki's flair stopped. She leaned toward the sure thing. Remember too, this is an old, conservative company. They're not into giving ambitious salesmen their head. They will likely cut him some slack even if there is not an immediate and huge result."

The group was back and Nikki resumed leading the meeting. "Okay, now that Brian is closer to the Cabo trip, who else is in the running?" She looked around the room and leveled her gaze on Liz, an attractive brunette. Her clothes were cutting edge professional. I noticed that she was very serious minded and had been taking notes during Brian's time.

"Well, Nikki, as you know I just landed a fairly substantial account and according to the art department the campaign is under way. While I feel pretty good about that what I'm having a problem with is my next target."

Nikki jumped in. "So your problem is prospecting. No new leads?"

"Exactly. I've tried all the old tried and true methods. Going back over old inquiries that never panned out. Watching the ads and commercials for what I feel are ineffective campaigns and going after them. Networking. I'm, frankly, out of ideas at this point."

I got the impression that Nikki fired from the hip. She quickly shot back, "Then all you can do is fall back on the salesperson's nemesis."

"You mean...?"

Everyone was grinning now. And as the grins grew and multiplied, Nikki shouted, "That's right, boys and girls, when everything else fails go to cold calling." All the grins had turned to laughter now and even Liz was laughing. Nikki continued, "Just put on your hiking shoes and make the rounds of companies. Get appointments, use your old sources. You're not new to the game, Liz. Hit the bricks if you have to, but get appointments. Remember you're in show business. You're only as good as your last hit." Everybody laughed at that too but it was a rather forced effort.

Rex turned to me. "She's not kidding, really."

The meeting resumed. A tall guy, Larry, a sharp dresser with a smug smile called out from the back, "Nikki, this is in the form of a beef. As you know I don't have any problems with my selling." Again the room erupted in guffaws and horseplay.

"Yeah right, Larry," they called.

"My beef is this: we go out and bust our butts to get an account that's into film. And what does the brass do? They put our West Coast office on it and come up with some has-been old actor from the seventies to star in a TV ad, selling the Boomers all kinds of financial products like life insurance and reverse mortgages. Sure, they might be fine for the geriatric crowd. They're solid citizen types. But put them in other types of commercials and as far as I'm concerned they bomb. No, I take that back, not as far as I'm concerned, but the books show that they bomb. I hate that. It makes short shrift of our efforts."

Nikki chuckled. "I got ya, Larry. But our job is to SELL. We have very little control of things after that. Oh yeah, we can make our recommendations but in the end we don't hold the purse strings. But on the other hand, ya gotta admit sometimes the creative types are able to put a shine on the sneakers we hand in to them. Admit it. Some pretty good things happen to some lackluster companies and products. So it is a two way street."

She peered around the room. "Okay gang, I guess that's it."

Before they could begin shuffling out, Nikki called out, "Oh yeah, one more thing. I'm going to suggest to the brass that we hold our sales meetings in one of the lounges at the Westin hotel once a month. Whaddya think?"

There was a very short pause and somebody called out, "Nikki rocks!"

Just about everybody there seemed to agree.

Rex and I were smiling when the room quieted down.

Now we hoped Nikki could give us some time. As she started

to walk over to us, her cell phone chirped. She picked up and listened. Stopping just in front of us she said into the phone, "Look honey. I'm sorry. I forgot all about that meeting with you at school. Is it too late to do anything about it? Oh, I see. Well again, I'm sorry. I'll store the info in my phone next time so I won't forget. What was that? Uh huh. Oh, I don't know, I guess I didn't get the whole story on that. See you at home. No. I'll be on time tonight."

Turning to us she grinned and added, "I hope."

She was about to say something when her cell chirped again. "Yeah. Cortez." She listened and then interrupted. "Shoot. Did I forget that? I'll get right on it."

She turned to us. "Gotta run. Hope I did you guys some good," and then she was gone. We heard the staccato of her heels hurrying down the hall.

"What do you think?" Rex asked me.

"A busy lady. A go getter," I said, adding, "maybe a bit 'out there' too."

"But," Rex noted, "probably very effective."

"And you're right," I said, recalling what he had told me earlier, "I do see some of the characteristics of the Driver type of leadership."

"Like the way she seeks practical solutions."

"And insists on getting results," I said.

"Yes, that poor girl who has been forced into cold calling," Rex said. "Though Nikki's suggestion may seem a bit harsh, the truth is, as sparse as those pickings might be, the company isn't paying their sales force to sit there and wait for their next sale to magically just walk through the door. They need to do whatever is necessary, even including things like cold calling, which salespeople sometimes find unpleasant."

"That seems like an understatement, Rex."

He just smiled, which I think was his understated way of telling me he was pleased that I was beginning to catch on. The different leadership styles became easier to identify the more time you spend observing them, and I was starting to feel more confident now after watching these other professionals in action.

TORCH LIGHT LEADER

By now I was really beginning to enjoy the little adventures that Rex was taking me on. It made me rather sad knowing that this was going to be one of our final times shadowing a person's workday to learn about their leadership style. But I was sure that it would be at least as productive as the previous three, which had each brought with them so much insight. I had never realized that I had so much to learn.

This time Rex and I visited JFK Memorial High School in suburban Boston. It was mid-June, balmy and graduation was near. We had an appointment with Mr. Frank Brewer, the school's Guidance Counselor, and we first met him for breakfast in the school cafeteria. Frank explained to us that the previous evening he had presented a Career Night in order to introduce the seniors to some of the options available to them after graduation. He had arranged for representatives from industry and from the armed forces to address students about their post-graduation plans. He told us that he thought the event went well, but it was important to reach out to the kids on a personal level, too, something that could never be accomplished quite the same way in a public setting.

From what I could tell so far, Frank Brewer was an amiable

sort of guy, and he seemed so calm, cool and collected that I could liken him to Mr. Rogers, the gentle soul of Children's TV. Except Brewer was livelier, and obviously had a more direct attitude.

Sipping his coffee he said, "I have to admit that this year's crop of students seem more informed than those in the past."

I asked, "Why do you think that is, Frank?"

"My guess," came his reply, "is that it's tied to the Internet and the explosion of technology."

Rex said, "How does that affect their career decisions?"

Frank seemed to have an answer ready without even having to think about it. "These kids have so many choices available to them, that the toughest challenge is helping them to get focused. That's how I see my job, encouraging them to discover what their real passion is, and then helping them to pursue it with whatever resources that might be available for them."

After breakfast we went to Frank's office to listen in on his follow-up interviews with the students. Rex and I sat in the back of the office and tried to remain as non-intrusive as possible.

The first session of the morning was with Lisa, a bubbly girl who greeted Frank with a happy smile. "I really liked the Career Night thing, Mr. B. I'm thinking a Public Relations career might be a good fit for me."

Returning her smile, Frank said, "Well, that can certainly be a very rewarding field, and there are plenty of great opportunities if you have the right training." He perused her transcript and said, "You're doing some fine work, Lisa. It looks like the only thing keeping you off the honor roll is a C in Algebra."

A look of doubt came over the young girl's face.

Frank didn't let that linger. "No need to get discouraged, Lisa. Remember back in your freshman year when you didn't think you could make the track team?"

Lisa nodded.

"I suggested you practice all year and try out in your sophomore year?"

Her face brightened a bit, recalling the memory.

Continuing, Frank said, "Well, as we both know you took my advice and became one of our school's top runners this past year."

She blushed a bit. "Yeah, you're right."

"Lots of kids struggle with Algebra, Lisa. I suggest you get some tutoring." Mr. Brewer took out a slip of paper and wrote down an email address and a phone number. Handing it to her, he said, "I have the perfect solution for you. This woman has brought numerous kids just like you from C's and D's to A's and B's. Hey, that rhymes..."

Lisa laughed.

Frank did too. I could see he was the type of man who really enjoyed interacting with the kids. "But seriously, give her a call, Lisa. I honestly believe that boosting your Algebra grade is the key to getting into a great college and preparing for a terrific career. And I believe that you've got what it takes to succeed."

With a smile, the student got up to leave. "Thanks a lot, Mr. B. I can't wait to go home and tell my mom what you said."

When she'd left the office I asked, "Frank, do you really think she has a chance?"

Without pause he replied, "Of course she does -- if she puts in a genuine effort. It's all a matter of getting them to believe in themselves and their own abilities."

"How can you be sure?" I asked.

"I'll take the time to get to know these kids, most of them for four years or more. Lisa is a bright girl, but until this year she had never really taken her studies very seriously. I think that the idea of a PR job seems glamorous to her, which is great. That makes it an ideal motivator for her to want to make the honor roll and boost her chances of getting into a top-rate college and ultimately landing her dream job."

After listening very carefully, Rex piped up and said, "I heard a stat the other day that said that about 75% of kids who go to college do not get a job in their major. What do you make of that?"

"Sadly, I'm sure that's true," Frank replied in a somewhat subdued voice, lightly tapping a pencil on the edge of his desk. "Especially when the economy goes into the tank like it is now. But I've got to believe that what I'm doing makes a difference in the lives of these kids, regardless of economic circumstances. In fact, I'm certain of it."

The next student, a very big youngster who almost certainly had to be a linebacker, lumbered in about a minute later and seemed to not even notice us. Frank motioned him to a chair and told him that we were interested in today's job market and to ignore us, which he seemed to have no trouble doing.

"I really enjoyed Career Night, Mr. Brewer, but there's never enough time in those things to get all your questions answered."

"I'll be happy to help, Eddie. What's your question?"

"Well, to be completely honest with you I think I'm too immature to go out and tackle college right now and I don't want my parents to struggle coming up with tuition money, so I was thinking of joining the Air Force."

There was silence in the room.

"This way," he continued, "I could get some training, learn to live on my own, and when I come out have the government pay for college if I still want to go. As it is, if I went to college I have no idea what I want to study, and I don't want to spend four years studying stuff I don't think I'll ever use."

The Guidance Counselor didn't answer right away. He seemed genuinely impressed by the thoughtfulness this young man had put into his plan. Then he said, "You may not feel mature enough to go to college, Eddie, but that's a very mature decision you are thinking of taking. It shows that you're reasoning like an adult already."

The big kid smiled at the compliment. "Well, I still have to think about it some more. But thanks for being so supportive."

When the boy had left the office, Frank looked at us and smiled. "When you get one that sounds motivated and on the right on track, it feels awesome and makes it all worthwhile. I don't think he really needed much advice at all. Just some reassurance."

We thanked Frank for allowing us to listen and learn. In the car I turned to Rex. "Do you think Frank Brewer is typical of educators today? He seems like such an easy-going guy, and I think he really does care about the kids."

Rex chuckled. "I don't think there's a cynical bone in his body. He's more of a realist who sometimes gets pessimistic about things that he can't fix. But he's reconciled to the realities of life, and knows how to make the best out of things."

"So in other words," I said, "with this type of leadership style, if they can remain amiable and concentrate on problem solving and understanding people on a personal, one-on-one level, then they can expect to succeed."

Rex smiled at me. "If you keep learning your lessons this well, my friend," he said, "you're not going to need me around much longer."

CAMPFIRE LEADER

The Campfire Leader is the type of leader that we should all aspire to be like. Just like a campfire, they are warm and inviting. Their leadership style lights up the surrounding area making it easy to spot them as a leader. Also like a campfire, we are drawn to these kinds of leaders. They have passion for leadership making them easy to trust, because you know that they care for your well-being.

Like adding wood to a campfire, this Leader knows that the importance of constantly adding to their survival skills. Resource tools like books and articles on leadership are part of the 'essential' preparation. But more importantly, lessons learned through personal experiences are essential to a Campfire Leader. They strive and aspire to develop into the best leader that they can be. They share their life lessons and experiences not to tell you what you do wrong, but as a guide to lead you. They know that demonstrating is the most effective way to train and lead.

It was a clear and sunny spring morning. I met Rex at the Black Falcon Lines pier in South Boston. There we found the *Azamara Journey*® , a premier, luxury ship from Azamara Club Cruises®. She had just docked and the dock workers were still busy tying her up securely and adjusting the gangway into position. This was a turnaround for the *Azamara Journey*® as they had only ten hours to take on passengers, restock, refuel, and clean the ship in preparation for a cruise to Bermuda and back to Boston.

Rex had explained to me that Captain Tysse was the epitome of the Campfire leader, that type of leader who through his compassion and warmth leads his people with strength and professionalism, yet never seeming soft.

I then learned a little of Captain Tysse's background. After completing a year at the Seaman Apprenticeship School, he started out as a deckhand on tankers, then joined the Norwegian Navy and later joined Merchant Marines and tankers. With a thorough knowledge of the sea and ships he finally aspired to command a major cruise ship.

We waited at the Security area and asked for the captain. Despite how busy he was, the Captain arrived promptly and greeted me with a firm handshake and kind smile. Then, the unexpected. Along with the handshake for Rex came a hug, professional, but still a hug. This seems to say something about the man.

At his suggestion he led the way and we followed. The first stop was below decks where we were given a glimpse of the enormous task that was already underway. Dockside was piled with tons of supplies waiting to be loaded. The officers and crew were all quite busy with their tasks. Each officer was in charge of a division, which had multiple departmental functions to perform. Additionally, they had a specific routine to accomplish to ensure the ship was run efficiently and the task at hand was to depart the dock on time. Passengers were disembarking with all the commotion that entails. Cars, taxis and limousines were awaiting the passengers as well as many friends and relatives there to greet the travelers.

"Each port has its own challenges for several reasons, including geography, local customs, local rules and regulations, labor situations and myriad of other variables," the Captain told us, and it seemed overwhelming to me how much responsibility this man carried.

As we were observing the frenzied activity below deck, the Food and Beverage Manager approached us. He was a short man with a balding pate, and he looked worried. With a friendly warm smile, the Captain said "What can I help you with, Juan?"

"Captain, I know how important getting our shipment of fresh Maine lobsters is for the 'Best of the Best 'dinner event but I'm afraid that they tell me they can't make the delivery in time. Something about rough weather out on the Grand Banks and the boats were delayed getting in. But that's not the worst of it. It could still get here on time but the delivery truck has broken down up in New Hampshire."

The Captain thought a minute and then said, "Didn't you once tell me that you had some friends in the delivery business?

"Yes, I do. And they owe me a favor. I think I'll call them and see if they can help me with this"

"Good job, Juan. That's the way to solve the problem."

After the young man had hurried off, I asked, "Why congratulate him...didn't you basically hand him the solution to the problem?"

The Captain grinned. "Depends on how you look at it. Sometimes when we have problems we focus on the impossibility of solving it. It's common for people to give up when they think there is no solution. I try to get them to focus on the 'can do' possibility. If I take credit for solving the problem then they become dependent on me to solve it for them every time. That's not the way I'd rather do it."

Rex and I exchanged a knowing glance. When our host stepped away for a moment to deal with something, I said, "I'm starting to see why the Captain is a Campfire leader. The people with problems don't fear telling him about it because he might blow up. Instead, they know they are going to get a friendly assist with their problem."

Rex replied, "Right. Many leaders tell their subordinates, 'Come to me whenever you have a problem. My door is always open.' But many look at that as a cliché with no real meaning and that when they tell the boss of their problem, the boss is going to have no patience with them and immediately rush to a negative judgment of them. That's what they're afraid of. That they will be judged as incompetent for problems that really aren't their fault. A Campfire leader gives them the confidence to search themselves for an answer and to not fear unreasonable wrath. Of course, some need a suggestion or two but the point is they're not afraid to come to the boss with a problem."

Later that evening after the ship had sailed, we were taking a tour of the ship. As we approached the bridge, a junior officer greeted us. The Captain introduced him to us but the man seemed distracted and grim – there was even a vague hint that he may even have been crying. The Captain ushered him aside, but they were still in earshot. The young officer told the captain his problem. As a new officer and new to the sea he found himself unexpectedly homesick. He had been away from home for over four months and now was facing two more months away. He admitted that he was having trouble coping.

Although very busy, the Captain paid attention to the young man's dilemma. He said, "You know, that is not unexpected. When I first went to sea I had the same problem, Jack."

The youthful officer stared at him. "You did?"

"Yes, everyone including seasoned sailors experience homesickness."

"How did you handle it?"

"Not a day goes by that I don't miss my lovely wife of fourteen years. And Bella, our precocious Mal-Tzu. But it's really a very natural problem with a very natural solution. When I am aboard ship, the crew, fellow officers and even sometimes passengers become my family away from home. I put time into relationships including all the problems that arise and just like the home family it is a challenge. Challenges consume the mind and before you know it you're home."

The man seemed dubious.

The Captain said, "I don't see you at any crew functions or gatherings or even at passenger events. Why is that?"

"I don't know for sure, sir. I guess I don't think about it as you just said, as if they're my family away from home. I just never got involved. Maybe my heart wasn't in it?"

"Well that's the trick, Juan. Get into it and make your shipmates part of your family. The key is to become involved. You will find that your fellow crew members all have the same kinds of problems and we can all help each other. You'll feel more connected knowing you have the backing and compassion of friends." After a brief pause, the Captain added, "Why don't you plan on going to crew's monthly birthday party? It'll be a good chance to mingle with some of the crew and maybe make new friends. In fact, we'll go together! Let's meet 10 minutes before at the Mosaic Café®."

Brightening, the man responded, "Thank you, sir. I'll take your advice. And I'm sorry to have bothered you at such a busy time."

The Captain smiled. "Nothing is more important than the wellbeing of my crew, Nothing."

The junior officer left with a spring in his step.

When the Captain rejoined us he said, "When I first went to sea I was told to be harsh, that command was all about discipline. I found that to be more an old tradition of the sea and Navy men than anything else. In the Cruise business, it is all about taking care of the passengers and showing them a good time, besides running the ship and being assured of its safety; which, naturally, is our foremost job. Of course I'm not saying that the boiler room personnel are responsible for the passengers' fun but we top senior officers certainly are. It doesn't matter if we have many stripes or no stripes, it all comes down to guest satisfaction! It's not good for morale to have a young officer moping about, seeming gloomy. It doesn't give the proper image, not to mention the reality of the poor man's unhappiness. I think he'll now make it his business to make friends and get involved with his shipmates. We all are integrated, like dominos. We can only succeed if we support each other."

We weren't on the busy bridge long when we ran into the First Officer. He too wasn't very happy. "It seems," he said, "that the Port Authority had a problem with our environmental report."

The Captain asked to see the Environmental Officer. A pretty young woman (who seemed rather perturbed) soon arrived. The Captain said, "Liz, I know you want to do the best job that you can on our Environmental reports. I know we've had problems in the past. What seems to be the main problem?"

"Well, sir," she said a bit flustered. "I usually just don't have enough time and on a short turnaround like this I definitely don't have enough time."

The Captain smiled warmly at the young woman. "You know, Liz, I once had your job. I know it's difficult. Let me tell you how I solved some of the problems, especially ones involving a fast turnaround like this one."

She listened intently and when the Captain was done she turned to him. "Well, thank you, sir. Those are things I hadn't thought of. I was just trying to go by the book, but these recommendations are very helpful. I'll do better, sir."

"I know you will. Let me suggest that I review your reports for the next couple of months so we can get through this together."

"That would be very helpful, sir."

"Good," he said with a smile. "I know you'll do a good job and it will reflect well on our ship as well as our whole company.

"Thanks," the young woman replied, "that will give me a lot more confidence knowing you have double checked me."

When the busy Captain again got called away to perform some duty, Rex and I had a chance to exchange our observations. I said, "Boy, he solves problems easily doesn't he?"

"Indeed. And, he always solves them with a smile. Not only on his face, but also in his voice which is the sign of a genuinely caring individual as well. That's why I wanted you to meet. He is as an example of a true Campfire leader."

Reflecting some more, Rex said, "You know, Jim, way back in the day I was in the Navy. And although the purpose of a Navy ship and the purpose of a cruise ship are of course quite different, something about life at sea is the same. I think the Captain hit the nail on the head in dealing with that homesick young officer. In the Navy if we didn't have our groups of friends, or even one good friend, I know I personally would have been lost. The days at sea seemed endless and one needed that human companionship to get by. I might not have received a smile and some good conversation from the Skipper, but I sure did from my buddies."

"I see," I said, as it was all making a lot of sense. "But it looks to me like the Captain's leadership style is not only paternal but friendly. Let's face the facts; the paternal could sometimes be harsh. It doesn't automatically come with a smile. The Captain, on the other hand, leads by serving his people. It goes beyond being paternal and friendly, it also includes professional advice, as we saw with the young woman officer."

"And remember, Jim," Rex said to me, "that is also a two way street. If he goes out of the way to help his subordinates, they will surely go out of their way for him."

The next morning, the Captain joined us for an early breakfast and we continued our conversation. He said, "I treat each person according to his temperament. We respect each race, sex, religion, culture and a ship is like a mini United Nations. We have anywhere from forty-five to fifty countries represented in our crew. And with that comes the importance of respecting your colleague and co-worker as an individual and equal partner. As for personalities, if he or she is a direct person that wants to lead, then I will stand beside them and offer them advice along the way. If they are more amiable and not quite as assertive, then I might show them how to do it first and then observe and always offer encouragement. So in that respect and to some extent I see myself as a teacher too. If you don't have other plans, I'd be honored to have you join us at our Bridge Officers lunch on the bridge together with the Steering Committee."

At noon, Rex and I joined Captain Johannes and the Bridge Officers for a fantastic meal set at a long table setup on the bridge. Johannes graciously introduced us to the few members that we had not met previously. Each time he told us something personal about the individual. One such example was when Johannes said "This is our Chief Engineer Geoff, from Liverpool. Geoff's family also resides in Boston. His hobby as a Master Gardner is a passion whenever he is home. And his extensive knowledge of plants is a great asset to our crew in both floral décor and our purchasing of vegetables and fruits."

Johannes not only thanked his officers for their time and service, but he publicly thanked the servers who setup the tables, chairs and all of the food and tablescape items. No job was too big or too small to be recognized and valued.

Later that evening I went to the Cabaret Lounge® to watch the show and Rex went to the Looking Glass® a little later that evening to see the late night comedy show. The 'Tribute to Broadway' was spectacular! But the amazing thing was we both witnessed Johannes interacting with a great many guests and crew. And I have to admit that I laughed when Johannes introduced the Cruise Director, Eric, as his "identical twin brother" when it was very evident by their physical appearances and accents that they could not have been more different.

Early the next morning we entered the port. As we exited the ship the Captain gave us each a hearty hug and we wished him "Bon voyage." As he walked away and waved good-bye he said "I hope to have you cruise with us again soon." To which Rex replied "Absolutely!"

And as we drove away from the port, Rex and I reflected on our journey. We both agreed that it had been a wonderful trip. I said to Rex, "There is one thing really stands out to me about a true Campfire leader."

"What would that be?" he asked.

"Well, he needs to be as effective and hard driving as any other officer but he has to lead and guide and motivate all the others."

Rex smiled. "Yes. But of course, the devil is in the details."

"True," I said. "Unlike other sea commands such as the Navy or the Merchant Marine where discipline is the main motivator, the Captain of a cruise ship needs to be a skilled leader with the instincts of a motivational speaker and the compassion and insights of a psychiatrist. His business, in fact, is just the opposite of a ship of commerce or a ship of war. The purpose is to show a couple of thousand vacationers a good time. Yet all of the problems and the rules of the sea and safety considerations prevail. It's quite a job."

"That's right," Rex confirmed. "I'd say a Captain on a cruise ship is up there with the CEO of a major corporation. And he has an even more awesome responsibility than the CEO, who is only responsible for making a profit. In addition to safety he has so many lives in his hands and he is responsible for making both his crew and passengers happy."

" Any personality style can effectively lead the ship. However, because of the diversity in nationalities and cultures it seems that a Campfire leader is best equipped for that task," I said.

Mr. Lloyd smiled. "I think you get it now, Jim," he replied. "I think you get it."

CONCLUSION

Rex and I met for lunch and to discuss our recent experiences regarding leadership. We found a quiet table in the back of a little coffee shop in downtown Boston. Our coffee came first and as Rex was stirring his he asked, "OK, Jim, so what was your general overall impression from all that we've seen together?"

I smiled. "It's funny and I don't know how this got into my head but it seems to me that it's lot like trying to find a good pair of shoes."

I got the expected raised eyebrows from him.

"Shoes?"

I laughed. "Yes. Hear me out. You know how when you're trying on shoes, there's more than just one factor to consider? I mean, you have to like the color, the style, the price, and, of course, it has to fit well too. It seems to me that leadership styles are in a certain way similar to that. You have to match the right qualities to the task at hand, just like it has to be just the right shoe for the person who is buying it."

Rex nodded and said, "I have to say, Jim, I've never quite heard it expressed that way, but I think that you might be on to something. Please continue."

I cleared my throat. "So, it seems to me that the industries, businesses and departments of business we looked at had found and helped to develop the kind of leaders that work best for their particle niche in commerce."

"Go on."

"Well, some of the qualities that some types of leaders had would not work in other fields yet worked perfectly in their own."

Rex seemed even more interested now. I'd learned how to see it in his eyes. "For example?" he asked.

"Well, take the first guy we met, the manager of a crew building a structure. He solved his problems because of his strengths of leadership. Mainly dynamic, with an active, compulsive need for change. He corrects wrongs, is strong willed and decisive. As I see it, he wasn't necessarily born with all those skills but learned some of them by osmosis because of his field. He wouldn't work well, for instance, as the ship captain we saw last. See what I mean?"

Rex considered it for a moment and then replied, "Yes, I think I do. What you're saying is that leadership skills are not all inclusive. Sure, the boss, manager or head of anything needs to lead, but they don't all have the same abilities and talents and the organizations that are successful have the right leader in the right job."

"Right. Or they wouldn't be half as successful and that really could mean failure in the competitive world of business."

"I see your point," Rex said. "But here's something else that I want you to keep in mind. Do you think it's possible for each kind of leader we've observed to become a true Campfire leader, and if so, how, considering some of the flaws we've seen?"

I sipped some of my coffee and thought about his intriguing question. Then I said, "Well, it seems to me that no one person will ever possess all of the best leadership qualities, and everyone will have at least a few negative traits. It's just part of being human. That's why being a keen observer of people's behaviors is so important. When you can pick up on the cues and signals that you're getting from others, you can adapt your own leadership style to whatever circumstances you might encounter in any given situation."

With a smile, Rex said, "Exactly! Remember our visit with the Captain the other day. His Environmental Officer couldn't keep up with the workload, and so he offered to teach her some ways to get her work in on time, thus alleviating her problem. He needed to show flexibility, and he did, based on his solid understanding of this other individual's style and competencies."

It was like a light bulb went off inside my head. I said, "I think I saw at least the potential for that kind of adaptability in all of the people that we visited, Rex, now that you mention it. For example, Nikki, the sales manager, was a classic Disco Light leader. She was great at telling stories and getting co-workers to be enthusiastic. But she could definitely afford to be a bit more logical. Her approach might not work with certain employees or clients."

"So she needs to be a little bit more like...?" Rex asked.

"I would say, more like a Lighthouse leader," I said.

"That would be Syndee, the Account Manager at the video game."

"Yes," I said. "She was very focused and analytical, and I know that served her well. That's the kind of logic I was talking about."

"But?"

I knew exactly where he was going with this. "But on the other hand she could have used a little more energy and enthusiasm. That was definitely lacking, and I could see how it might present some problems for her when it comes to getting along with others on an interpersonal level."

He continued, "Jim, I am impressed. What about the Torch leadership style. What did you see as the pluses and minuses there?"

I had to think back... "Oh yes, that would have been Frank Brewer, the Guidance Counselor. I really liked him. The way he was involved with those kids' lives and genuinely cared from them was actually inspirational. On the downside, it seemed like he had a lot of trouble being direct with people."

"There is a time for being direct," Rex said.

"Yes," I agreed. "I know that's probably not something that comes to him naturally, but to be even more effective in his job, to be a true Campfire leader, he might need to work on that a little bit."

I was of course seeing the clear pattern now. Each one of these leadership styles displayed traits that could help leaders in their prospective careers, but they also had inherent flaws that if they pinpointed them and did the necessary work, could make them even more successful.

"The one other person we had visited was a typical Strobe light kind of leader, and that would bring us back to where we began, with Jake Simpson, the architect."

"What did you make of him?" Rex asked.

"Well, on the one hand he was certainly a take charge kind of guy. I could see that he liked to give commands and exert his authority."

"Did that approach seem to work for him?"

I replied, "I suppose, yes, on a certain level it did. But he needs to be organized and exhibit more passion for being an actual leader. That means knowing how to guide people, not just ordering them around."

Mr. Lloyd finished his coffee and said, "Jim, it seems to me that you're really connecting all of the dots now. Any other thoughts you'd care to share with me?"

I smiled, as his approval meant a lot to me. "Yes, one more thing, and I think I'm going to have to return to my shoe analogy. There really is no 'one size fits all' approach when it comes to leadership," I said.

"Precisely!" he said, waving his hand for emphasis. "The best leaders realize this, and they know how to apply the right skills to each situation. That way, when dealing with others they know how to take their particular abilities or talents and show people how to maximize their potential. Those are the kinds of leaders who can move mountains."

"And make it look easy," I added.

"Strong leadership is never easy," my wise friend advised. "But, if taught properly and practiced consistently, eventually it does become a part of you. It becomes an engrained way of seeing the world, and of conducting yourself in it."

"Well," I said, looking across the table in admiration, "if I've been half as good a student as you've been a teacher, I've got nothing to worry about."

"I couldn't have said it better myself," Mr. Lloyd quipped. And we both shared a good laugh.

ABOUT THE AUTHOR

Rob Jackson is the President of Magnovo Training Group, an internationally requested keynote speaker and professional development trainer. He lives in Indianapolis, IN with his family but proudly hails from Salinas, CA.

Rob enjoys traveling, scuba diving and most of all making a difference in the lives and careers of individuals.

Upcoming books by Rob include:

Campfire Communicator

Sea-Level Executive

www.Magnovo.com

FOR MORE INFORMATION

To learn more about this subject, or to find out how to book Rob Jackson for a keynote please go to our website at:

www.CampfireLeadership.com

www.ingramcontent.com/pod-product-compliance
Lightning Source LLC
Chambersburg PA
CBHW041717200326
41520CB00001B/135